CHANGE
THE CONVERSATION

Letting Go of Thoughts that Hold Us Hostage

January 2013

Dear Sister Maureen,

Thank you for your
truth, love and Courage
in ministering to
change so many
conversations!

Blessings,
Nan

CHANGE
THE CONVERSATION

Letting Go of Thoughts that Hold Us Hostage

Nan Brenzel, Ed.D.

My Heartfelt Gratitude
To
Harleigh Gordon
For his gift of insight in creating my book cover
Email: Funk1ind@live.com
Funk1 Industries
http://funk1ind.com/

www.bookstandpublishing.com

Published by
Bookstand Publishing
Morgan Hill, CA 95037
3466_7

ISBN 978-1-61863-037-7

Printed in the United States of America

~ In Memory ~

Of

Fawn, my Way Home

~ Filled with Gratitude for your Grace and Love ~

John J. Adams

Jerry Eppler

Kari Z. Goldberg

Brenton MacKinnon

Sr. Mary Neill

Ralph J. Pinkerton

ACKNOWLEDGEMENTS

~The Secret is not how to begin but how to begin again~

Thank you my brothers and sisters of faith. You have relentlessly cleared my path and stood with me whenever my memories threatened reality, created paranoia or manifested delusion. Your wisdom, courage and support help me to identify the cues and triggers operating in my own thoughts and actions.

I have emerged whole and alive into love and light. I have jailed the demons and now live in this healing oasis called the Present. My feelings, thoughts and actions are deeper than I remember.

I did not have a choice then.

I do have a choice now.

My Spirit has never abandoned me.

CONTENTS

x

INTRODUCTION

Dear Reader,

Why a handbook?
CHANGE THE CONVERSATION is a handbook for those determined to grow out of negative thoughts, habits and actions resulting from cultural patterns, natural conditioning and even programming. This handbook maps a way out by identifying your Present Self whose focus is to stay mindful in the present moment.

Why write a handbook now?
This work is a call to the collective to radically examine any and all possibilities and experiences you can share and contribute to our world becoming a more positive place. It invites each of you to identify and name your past so that you can move freely ahead and more fully embrace your Present Self.

What is the basis for the information in this handbook?
The information presented in this handbook originates from three sources: my personal experiences, the experiences of my clients and my life long study of conditioning, programming and spirituality. In my career of helping people to transform distressful life styles and from my intense personal work, I have found common threads in the processes of conditioning, programming and extreme programming. This handbook presents skills to help you reclaim and define yourself in the present.

An Invitation

Faith not Fear
Before you begin reading this handbook, I ask that you consider a faith contract. This is the same powerful pledge and agreement with those I have supported on this journey. Our power originates from an indefinable source within that has kept us all alive. If you find you cannot sign this page today, revisit it as you read through the handbook.

Dear Present Self,

This is a written commitment promising you my love, regardless of what I may remember. I honor you regardless of what you may have been or done as you are my first and foremost gift to the world.

I will comfort you, protect you, release you and accept you under all circumstances and in all situations. My heart was broken, my Soul restricted and my body abused. Yet, my Spirit was untouchable and could not be driven away or defeated. I still bear scars. I am ready for surgery. My love for you is now unconditional. Just as I practice understanding of those whom I love, let me bathe you in warmth and caring.

I am free now in my mind, my heart, my body and my Soul.

_____   _____

           Signature   *Date*

How to Use this Handbook

You already have all that you need to identify past and present experiences that relate to conditioning, programming, cues and triggers. The goal of CHANGE THE CONVERSATION is to provide a sequential format with building blocks to assist you in creating a personal structure to identify and remain in your Present Self. The Present Self is the person within us who is in contact with, experiences and identifies feelings, thoughts and actions in the current moment. This is the dominant part of our persona, living in the moment and in the Now of life.

CHANGE THE CONVERSATION handbook uses first person pronoun "I" and "me" in each section so that you can identify with or reject a concept based on your personal experience. The following format is used throughout this handbook to assist in self exploration:

Noticing & Awareness
This is your noticing and awareness section. It points out feelings, thoughts or actions you may or may not be aware of in your everyday life. It asks you to begin noticing your surroundings. Read the *Noticing & Awareness* section first to determine if you want to read the passages on that page. Each page includes notes or hints on what to do if you experience a trigger or uncomfortable feeling.

The Thought
These are past ideas or beliefs, both natural and programmed which can prevent you from identifying and remaining in your Present Self.

The Notion
This section presents ideas, conditioning and programming from the past. Coupled with the introduction of a new thought or a variation in approach, this will assist you in moving towards a more vibrant and Present Self.

The Way Out

In this section, ideas are presented to identify, assess, control, break or eliminate unwanted conditioning, coding and/or triggers used to set in motion a personality or behavior.

The Meditation

This is a process to introduce a present and current experience. You will anchor consciousness in your Present Self and allow for new experiences in the present and the future.

Journaling

Writing and recording experiences as you use this handbook helps to create your personal code book for living life fully in the present. Write notes in this handbook and/or use a separate journal.

The information contained in this handbook offers suggestions and possibilities for opening to a present condition of freedom in living. It is not meant as a stand alone self help guide or as a substitute for clinical intervention.

Useful Skills for Changing the Conversation

The four elements that teach you to change the conversation are: awareness, interruption, substitution and practice.

Awareness. This is your ability to notice what is taking place around you and your ability to stay aware of your behavior, thoughts and feelings in the present moment. Awareness requires that you focus on just two factors. What has lead up to the present moment and makes you feel noticeably uncomfortable? What sensations are you experiencing that do not support how you want to be in the present?

Interruption. This is the act of breaking into a thought pattern that uninterrupted, would lead to an undesired and/or inappropriate past behavior. You can think of these thought patterns as a chain reaction. You must break the chain. There is a simple technique for interruption.

> This is the **STOP Technique**. It is done by verbally or mentally shouting out the word STOP as forcefully and lovingly as you can. Verbal is stronger than mental but it may not always be socially acceptable.
>
> Use the **STOP Technique** as soon as you become aware of any thought or feeling that you have historically responded to with undesirable or inappropriate behavior.

By using the **STOP Technique,** the thought pattern linking your chain reaction is broken and your mind is open to substituting an alternative and new thought or behavior. At first you may find the STOP Technique interrupts your thought pattern only momentarily. You may have to use the technique repeatedly and in rapid succession to keep an unwanted thought or behavior from reoccurring.

Substitution. To successfully change behavior, interruption must be linked with substitution. Substitution is the act of choosing a desirable alternative thought or behavior in place of an undesirable thought or behavior. There are three areas of behavior in which substitution is applicable: things that you do (action or activity), things that you think (thought) and things that you say or imagine (speech).

The more mentally and physically you can become involved and the longer the action lasts during substitution, the more effectively it will prevent a lapse into the past. Your next most frequently used substitution technique focuses on what you think. Changing your conversation refers to replacing negative destructive thoughts (often from the past) with positive, constructive thoughts in the Present Self.

Practice. Repeat steps one through three: Awareness, Interruption and Substitution, over and over again until they become part of your present everyday life.

THE HABITS

My past experiences, deeply encoded thoughts, triggers, cues, suggestions, ideas or actions.

I now create new habits that support my Present Self.

The Thought

Eight basic conditions of a habit form the groundwork to help control and/or eliminate conditioning and programming.

Noticing & Awareness

Make a check mark next to any of the basic conditions of a habit that feel more charged for you than others. Don't worry if you check them all.

The Notion

You may already know the basic conditions of habits. Some of you may become fearful and frustrated reading and hearing about them. Some of you may be downright angry with them. Let's review the basic conditions in a way that you will begin to lay a foundation for making sense of some of life's experiences.

The Way Out

There are eight basic conditions associated with a habit:

- Momentum: a habit gains momentum each time it is practiced.
- Reversion: the tendency to revert to a familiar and often unproductive habit increases when I am tired, hungry, stressed or angry.
- Awareness: noticing the habit so that I know it exists.
- Short-circuiting: learning which of my thoughts and behaviors lead up to an unproductive habit allows me to short-circuit them by changing the conversation.
- Decisions: changing or discarding a habit isn't always about my behavior; it is about a decision to not engage in an unproductive or past thought.
- Selectiveness: some of my habits just need to change; all of my behavior does not need to change.
- Practice: habits are predictable and can be changed with committed, even relentless practice. Practice is a lifelong art.
- Trust: all the education in the Universe won't necessarily make a difference for some habits. Sometimes it is a matter of just trusting the process.

The Meditation

Habits are best understood by journaling with both the left and right hand. I can learn about the past and the present by recording stories about habits.

Never use a computer until you are ready to record what your hands have written. You only need to write and to notice.

Notes

The Thought

Momentum: A habit gains momentum each time it is practiced.

Noticing & Awareness

When I remain in blame, I can perpetuate a cycle of blame, attack, victim and rescue. Without interruption of my thoughts or actions I risk taking on a full time victim mentality.

The Notion

It is difficult to define the beginning of a habit and almost completely impossible to attach a sole cause for the habit. Many painful hours are spent searching for the "reasons." I see, know and feel the games and yet I have become a victim of the habit.

The trap is I am locked into blame and my current events so deeply that I believe I have no right or ability to gain control. I may be blaming "them" and of course I feel I "should." It is these very reactions that continue to feed my helplessness.

The programming is that when I feel victimized, I seek a way out at all costs or a more comfortable way just to "please" someone else. I can then fail to control or eliminate the habit because I am in conflict with what I intuitively know and can no longer justify responding to with blame.

The Way Out

I agree to give up blame.

The cycle of blame can turn into anger.

This cycle leads to limited or no control over everyday situations in the present. The past, when allowed a free reign of blaming energy, continues its invisible grip over how I nourish my Present Self.

Granted, there can be intense pain in the past. If I continue to give the past power by reinforcing these memories, I will never experience and enjoy the full positive life I have been missing.

The Meditation

I notice who and what I continue to blame for my past. I notice when my thoughts and language use past tenses. I focus on thoughts and actions that help me to stay in the present.

Three thoughts that help me stay in the present are:

1. _____

2. _____

3. _____

Notes

The Thought

Reversion: The tendency to revert to a familiar and often unproductive habit increases when I am tired, hungry, stressed or angry.

Noticing & Awareness

Use the STOP Technique as desired.

Either keep a journal or carry a notepad and pen with you. People have been known to lose their journals and notes during the change process. You may even want to send a trusted friend an email to remind you of where you keep your journal and notes.

The Notion

Stress, hunger, lack of sleep and anger evoke a chemical change in my body. Chemical changes trigger responses. There is a brief moment where I can fully and knowingly recognize this chemical change. Up until now I may have interpreted this as "oh, no, here it comes" or I may have developed some technique to short-circuit it or even go unconscious and not remember. The trap is not the trigger or pattern, the trap is the decision I make about not staying in the noticing.

I may not even be aware that I am making a decision. I need to remain aware. Always aware - not vigilant - that is different. Awareness is the key to short-circuiting patterned responses.

The Way Out

I am listening to the early cues my body sends me.

I can use the STOP technique to interrupt a cue at anytime. The earlier I recognize a sequence of cues, the more of an opportunity I have to interrupt the process and short-circuit the undesirable end result.

The Meditation

I remain aware of the changes in my body by keeping a journal of what happens just before and after I have a past memory. I trust I will learn the early cues and signals from my body and stay in my Present Self.

Some bodily cues and signals I am aware of now:

_____

_____

_____

_____

_____

_____

Notes

The Thought

Awareness: I stay in the noticing and awareness of what precedes or triggers the habit.

Noticing & Awareness

Some common every day items in my environment can trigger thoughts and actions. Unless I can identify what the item specifically triggers, I am prepared to throw out or give away any item I identify as a trigger.

The Notion

As I learn to identify which behaviors lead up to or trigger an unproductive or destructive action, I can short-circuit it by productive self-talk directed to the Present Self.

The Way Out

To eliminate negative visual triggers, I plan to take an inventory of my entire house, workspace, car and other places I frequent.

I look around at each item and trust my gut to tell me if I feel a trigger or anything that feels like familiar conditioning or programming. I eliminate these items when possible by placing them in a box or brown bag or by throwing them out.

If I cannot eliminate an item, I slowly identify what it triggers and make note so that I can remain aware. I make notes in my journal about what I think or feel if I cannot remove a trigger item.

The Meditation

I will notice without judgment and reasonably remove any unproductive trigger(s) from my sight. Each day I sit in one room of my home and slowly look at each item in that room to see if I sense a trigger. I remember trigger items can be anything and may not appear to have any logical order or reasoning.

Notes

The Thought

Short Circuiting: To change or discard a habit I need to be aware of the habit and all the properties surrounding the habit.

Noticing & Awareness

When surrounded by multiple triggers, I may become extremely tired or extremely agitated for what seems like no apparent reason.

I am able to identify unconscious and programmed triggers if I begin to notice my surroundings with the intention of becoming aware of possible triggers.

To reduce exaggerated feelings, I use journaling to begin recording what cues and triggers are in my surroundings.

The Notion

Noticing increases my ability to recognize when I am approaching a limit and am about to engage in a self-destructive thought or behavior. I cannot change a behavior that I do not acknowledge exists. I do not need to know, understand or worry where this behavior originated.

Noticing simply means noting.

I am not required to analyze it, alter it or even stop it. Notice it. Notice where I am, who I am with, and the content of my inner conversations. I will wear a watch so I know how long I spend noticing or disappearing. I notice what patterns begin to emerge under what similar circumstances.

Noticing consists of increasing my awareness about my thoughts, feelings, moods, actions, hunger sensations, physical wants, comfort needs or inconsistencies in my responses to my environment. I will soon notice predictable patterns. I will not even try to make sense of these. I stay in the noticing.

The Way Out

Patterns equal how I change or adjust my behaviors to get something I knowingly or unknowingly need to get my "job" done or to reach my goal. Tracking through noticing and journaling my experiences helps me to stay in my Present Self.

The Meditation

I journal or write in my notes what my gut tells me feels wrong in my surroundings. Each time I experience an awareness of something taking place that is not consistent with the direction or decision I have made or feel I have made, I write it down and track it. In time, I see the threads to any conditioning or programming.

Notes

The Thought

Decisions and Selectiveness: I live in the willingness to release the habit and accept it back if it is useful. I am selective.

Noticing & Awareness

If I experience past thoughts then I return to my present surroundings and remind myself what I was doing. I write down any gut feeling(s) I have that may have triggered the lapse into the past.

The Notion

My willingness to carry my past fears ahead to the present forces me to stay in a constant state of surveillance. It requires that I must watch for attack from all sides and that I must pre-think and therefore predestine my future. It means I must strengthen my forces in case of attack.

As a result, I have forever determined my inaction around similar or like situations. Stepping out of "control" means I accept that I have both irrational and rational fears that others may not even find plausible. These fears resulted from thoughts, behaviors and actions I now find unacceptable. I am not unacceptable; however, there are parts of my past behavior that are no longer acceptable.

The Way Out

Changing or discarding a habit isn't always about the thought, behavior or action; it is always about a decision whether or not to engage in an unproductive or past memory. If I experience an unpleasant to frightening past thought, I immediately use the STOP technique, refocus on what I was doing in the present and say to myself, I can remain in my Present Self.

The Meditation

I am starting today. I am here now. I release my past judgments. The present offers what I desire and this is where I want to be. I say aloud the result(s) I want now. It is not necessary to have a plan to get there.

Some results I want now are:

_____

_____

_____

_____

Notes

The Thought

Practice: Habits are predictable and predictably unpredictable and can be altered with relentless practice. Practice is a lifelong art.

Noticing & Awareness

The word "stairs" or the thought of stairs may trigger a sense of sleepiness if hypnosis or programming was paired with descending a set of stairs. If I feel sleepy or remember stairs as a trigger word, I can skip to The Meditation section and then try reading The Notion later.

The Notion

The way in is the way out. I was made to climb down the stairs, the way out for me means I use the same track, tricks, traps and thinking to climb up the stairs. Fears can keep me away from the very tools that can open the present and allow me to live freely. I am willing to look into my past without fear that I will repeat acts I no longer believe are right and just. I start by defining what I desire and then stay consistent in what I feel, say, do, think and imagine.

The Way Out

Practice means consistency, not perfection. I practice releasing the habits of my past until I feel the consistency of what I say, what I want and what I do to get it.

I will listen to myself when I speak about my intentions:
- Am I saying what I want?
- Am I still telling myself what I don't want, can't have or can't do?
- Do I sound kind and encouraging to myself?
- Can I see myself having what I want?

I see it, feel it, think it, speak it and then listen to see if I am consistent. I use the STOP technique to quiet any chatter from past voices.

The Meditation

Before me is a long fence-like wall of plastic wrap. It stretches as far as I can see in both directions. I stand on one side. It is my life, as I know it now. The other side is my history/my past. I can push and pull this wall and it absolutely will not tear. Although I can see everything, nothing can leak through now. Nothing in my history or my past has the strength of my Present Self. I know the past and my history will always be there, transparent to me alone. I am living in this time - capable of making the decisions I want in the present.

Notes

The Thought

Trust: All the education in the Universe won't necessarily make a difference for some habits. Sometimes it is a matter of just trusting the process.

Noticing & Awareness

I may fear finding too many selves if I really listen. If my fear is overwhelming or I experience a fear I cannot identify, it is okay to skip this section completely.

The Notion

Most of us generally do not accept that it is our thoughts that lead us to an action. Programmed or not, actions originate in my thought domain. I want a reason to stop, a cause, someone or some situation to blame. Then it can all be justified. There will never be a justification for programming. It happened. I will open to the idea that emotional and psychological despair can be valuable.

Change, no matter how many professionals I seek, may not happen until I learn to turn down the volume on my self-talk. This may trigger a fearful response, because I might hear many voices inside my head. And the fear might be: What if I start to release this stuff and I don't have a "self" in there?

The Way Out

- Take nine (9) slow deep breaths. You are in there!
- I remind myself that I do have a Present Self in here.
- The way out is to turn down the volume and listen for my own voice.

I trust I am in there. I am gentle with myself when I feel anger or shame. Anger and shame will cause my voices to escalate. The goal is to work to gradually turn the volume down a little every week.

The Meditation

I have a voice of my own and I can find it by staying in the present. My voice is that of my Present Self.

Notes

THE THOUGHTS

Silent reminders of my past experiences. Focused words supporting my present direction and dreams.

My heart's desire supports all my Present Self thoughts.

The Thought

My duty was programmed, my desire is willful.

Noticing & Awareness

Write down your definition of duty and desire. First write using your dominant hand and then write the definition using your non-dominant hand. Compare similarities and differences in your definitions.

The Notion

If I were purposely conditioned or programmed, I may feel that "they" will always have some level of control. I may feel subjected to "others" for life. It is vital that I remind myself that I have a choice in the present and my future regardless of my past.

The Way Out

Duty has always equaled diversion and distraction from my Present Self's desires and needs to perform the will of others. Desire is the will of my Present Self.

The Meditation

Without taking too much time to think, answer the below:

My heart's desire is:

_____

_____

_____

_____

_____

_____

_____

_____

Post this somewhere you will read everyday for the next 30 days. If you feel creative add a poem, a song or even a collage.

Notes

The Thought

I simply cannot continue down a spiritual path struggling to stay "in control". It is bigger than that.

Noticing & Awareness

Please use your personal term and definition for a higher positive source outside yourself or for a higher source within yourself. The focus is to let go of control and turn down the volume on hyper-vigilance.

The Notion

There is only one situation where I have control and that is at the ground of my spiritual foundation. It lies in the basic assumptions that I make about myself (selves) and my relationship to life outside my "selves".

Growth on a spiritual path is trusting that all is working for my good. It is a true leap of faith. It is not meant to be done alone. What I am afraid of persists and recreates itself as if it were scripted for me personally until I am ready to accept control in the present.

The Way Out

I just need to believe there is another option besides the one I currently know and then trust that option.

The Meditation

Each day I remember that I can begin again as many times as I need to begin.

My current question about today is:

_____

_____

_____

_____

_____

Notes

The Thought

The way out of control is not always equal to the way I was conditioned or programmed into control.

Noticing & Awareness

Notice if any of the words in The Notion section have ever evoked an unusual bodily sensation. Make notes in your journal or the Notes Section.

The Notion

In purposeful programming there are formulae for splitting personalities and creating dissociative disorders. In some mind control programs and in severe cases of child abuse, words that have universal positive meanings in regard to how one interacts with a child were used to confuse and condition behavior. Thus, a child had confused feelings and conditioned fears in anticipation of their interaction when they heard the following words:

- The word Mommy could mean punishment or a threat.
- The word Daddy can have the dualistic meaning of punishment and reward, thus creating confusion by eliciting an unpredictable response.
- The word God generally means a reward. However, in programming the word could also mean a master, controller, programmer or handler.

If a child was continually abused and then conditioned to respond with confusion about the meanings of Mommy, Daddy and God, a major split could be created and triggered anywhere, accidentally and without anyone noticing.

The Way Out

Family constellations repeat themselves - meaning anyone perceived as Mommy, Daddy or God can have the same triggering process.

Notice: does anyone in my life space (including work) trigger me unintentionally as a result of my thinking of them as "family"?

I will note if I have markedly different behavioral patterns in the presence of my past memory of "family", blood family, friends, coworkers and even strangers.

The Meditation

There is more to me than my past. Inside my mind and body live a family of personalities. Many of these personalities are loving in the true spiritual sense of the word. I willfully chose to invite my real loving family (not always my blood family) to join me in my Present Self.

Notes

The Thought

I do not need fixing. My past brings me to this day and who I am now.

Noticing & Awareness

I am not a project, I am a person. Everybody has an idea on how to fix me. I do not need to be fixed. I become aware and identify the triggers. I turn down the volume of the false voices and directions inside and move forward. I have the ability to become more than my past.

I notice when I feel emotionally and physically hyper-vigilant. I check to be sure there is no immediate danger. I note in my journal who, what, where triggered the sense of hyper-vigilance. I revisit that part of my journal when I feel strong and I can review each situation slowly.

The Notion

Circumstances do not always dictate behavior. Many of us find ourselves engaged in performing tasks that have little or nothing to do with what we planned or imagine our real self to be. How many times have I looked in the mirror for someone else...and some days it could be anyone else?

On days when I sense this familiar struggle for control when there is none to be had I have an unexplainable willingness to participate in berating myself for an unknown reason. My memories of past behaviors often bleed through and I look for the "fix." I may have been labeled schizophrenic, paranoid, a liar and a loser. I know hyper-vigilance like my best friend's secrets.

The Way Out

When full, partial or flashback memories create an uncomfortable thought and/or feeling totally unrelated to the present moment I am experiencing, I remind myself that my task at this very second is to remain in the present. I will use the STOP technique to interrupt the memory and then refocus on where I am and what I am doing.

The Meditation

While I may only have partial memory or fleeting images of why I experience life as I do, my goal is to return to my Self in the present. I am able to experience a loving, full life in the present. Each day in my Present Self I create new experiences and memories. I know how to put old memories into a container. No one has a right to ask me to relive any of these memories.

Notes

THE COMMITTEE

A collection of multiple voices and/or healthy voices everyone hears in their head at times. Sometimes the committee includes the voices I hear inside my head that resulted from conditioning and/or programming.

My Present Self is in charge of my Committee.

The Thought

There are always, I repeat, always, voices speaking.

Noticing & Awareness

Hearing discussions inside my head is normal. These healthy voices assist me in an internal dialogue valuable in working through ideas. For highly programmed individuals, however, the voices can have a pre-coded message that maintains the same sequence of words to trigger a program or group of predetermined behaviors.

Continue to read this section, if you notice you feel uncomfortable, do not use your non-dominant hand to identify committee members.

The Notion

All people have a committee of conversations in their heads. It is a useful and healthy challenge to assist in working through ideas and plans. Programmed committees were intentionally built for specific jobs and can be triggered by anything to override common sense and self preservation.

The Way Out

I can clear away the debris that clogs my ability to hear the truth.

Draw a dozen circles around the oval below. With your non-dominant writing hand and without taking time to think about it or stopping to judge, write names and/or titles of your committee members around the oval. Use additional sheets in your journal as needed if you need more room for your committee.

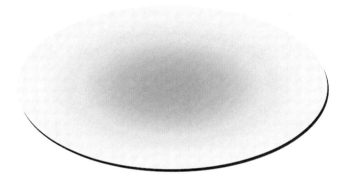

In the center of the oval (table) using your non-dominant writing hand, add words that describe your committee's tasks. Free flow your words; do not stop to make judgments.

The Meditation

I am in charge of the committee that speaks in my head. I control the committee by saying what results my Present Self wants. I can add or eliminate committee members whenever I desire.

Notes

The Thought

I can learn to manage the committee in my head with my Present Self.

Noticing & Awareness

The words, "Chief, Manager, Chair, Department Head, President" or similar titles for those in charge of a committee may trigger a response other than the usual definition of these words. If this is true in your history, begin reading this section at The Way Out. Try the entire section at another time.

The Notion

Being in charge of the committee is not my primary goal. These titles are connected to conditioning. The goal is for my Present Self to be in control, direct the conversations and be the loudest voice on the committee.

The Way Out

I will use a skill called regrouping. I make two lists.

List One: What matters now, in the present?

_____

_____

_____

_____

List Two: What doesn't matter now, in the present?

_____

_____

_____

_____

The Meditation

My intention and attention is solely focused on what matters to me now, in the present. Whenever I feel I am not in the present I simply repeat- I am in the Present Self now.

Notes

The Thought

I am committed to having new conversations with others and the committee voices in my head.

Noticing & Awareness

This section introduces the concept of reframing. Here's how it works. You say something that you know has just set off a trigger and you immediately recognize the familiar road this thought is going to take you down. Use the STOP technique by gently saying STOP. Then ask yourself: how can I say this in a different way in the present? If you stay in the trigger, write the words down in your journal. Then on occasion return to those words and see if you can come up with a new way of saying the same thing. Be patient, reframing is a slow process and practice is the key element. If you can stay in the awareness that this thought needs reframing, you will be making terrific progress.

The Notion

When I repeat stories of the wounds, I reinforce genetically and purposeful conditioned and/or programmed responses. I can change or eliminate the stories and my responses to the stories.

The Way Out

New language supports new thoughts, feelings and actions. I identify my trigger words and put them in the trash bin.

The Meditation

I release. I realize. I receive. I revise.

Notes

The Thought

I can learn to vibrate above the chatter of the committee and all other internal and external sounds.

Noticing & Awareness

Vibrating above or below a sound is as natural as breathing. And it is a technique that can stop sounds from setting off a trigger and help to eliminate excruciating headaches associated with slipping away from your Present Self.

If you are not a student of the energy modalities or do not believe in auras, then simply hum to yourself out loud. If you believe in the ability to impact the energy field around your body, then research musical notes and color.

The Notion

I either have forgotten or have a fear of remembering that I can vibrate above or below any frequency. This can be learned and used when internal sounds, the committee talk, or external noises or sounds trigger a warning system that I have slipped from the present. I recognize this is occurring when I sense that familiar feeling that something does not fit with what should logically be taking place.

The Way Out

Attention + Intention + Thought + Feeling + Action = Manifestation

Manifestation = the ability to develop Universal Connections

Universal Connections = Vibrational Changes

I work with trusted sources who understand auras, energy fields and sound therapy.

The Meditation

I am living in the way I want to be in the present.

My Spirit Self is the color violet and the musical note B. I will hum a song that feels healing and produces a feeling of well being.

Notes

THE SCRIPTS

Conditioning, programming, triggers and cues are often designed as intricately related patterns and can be activated by people, innate objects, signals, language or movement.

I can notice and change my thoughts and behaviors.

The Thought

I know the meaning of autopilot. I do, however, often forget where the plane is headed.

Noticing & Awareness

Many people cannot wear watches. This is an advantage for conditioning or programming because not wearing a watch forces one to easily lose sense of time. Carry a watch in a pocket, in a purse or brief case. Stay committed to checking the time regularly especially if there is a gut feeling of time slipping away or there is a noticeable lapse of time missing from the day.

The Notion

I may not be able to undo the conditioning or programming processes because of the intricate layering and threads. I can, however, anticipate, assess, control and break out of my conditioned responses.

The Way Out

I seek to understand and control one thought, one idea, one behavior or one action at a time. I wear a watch and note how long I can focus on what I am doing in the present. I write it down if necessary.

The Meditation

I am no longer trapped in a "no win" situation.

I see two squares; one has a warm fuzzy carpet and the other mounds of burning coals. I no longer have to choose pain to survive. I am now capable of separating the two. I chose the warmth of light and love.

Five ways I chose to feel loved:

1. _____

2. _____

3. _____

4. _____

5. _____

Notes

The Thought

I may not know the recipe. What I do know is that all recipes can be modified.

Noticing & Awareness

Many of us have desperately tried to fit in and then isolated ourselves for fear of being seen.

Today I will sense my place in the world as I am now.

The Notion

There are formulas and recipes. If I was purposely conditioned or programmed, I am wired differently from others. I sometimes feel a conflicting expectation that others might understand me, coupled with a fear and guardedness hoping they will not see the real me.

The Way Out

One plus two does not equal three in the conditioning and programming worlds.

I can expect unusual responses anywhere, anytime with anyone. As I learn the early cues and triggers, I learn to stay more firmly in my Present Self.

The Meditation

I am doing my best all the time. I do not have to repent for something that I may have done as an altered self. I do not know that personality nor would I chose it if I had full consciousness to say no.

Notes

The Thought

I do not know many others who are capable of understanding and nourishing my many "selves."

Noticing & Awareness

If you decide to do the exercise of left hand/right hand writing, you may trigger memories. It is critical to use self talk here and to tell your Present Self to just notice the changes. Use the STOP technique if you feel a trigger or feel a pull away from your Present Self. Repeat to yourself: I am remaining in my Present Self and will notice. I can stop this anytime I desire and go do something else.

If you feel triggered at any time, skip straight to The Meditation section.

The Notion

My fantasy is that someone outside of me will fix, save and understand me. If only I can explain it clearly enough without sounding insane, others won't think I am crazy.

The Way Out

I will find at least two people who refuse to call me crazy (paranoid, whacked, etc.). I will call one friend everyday. I will ask him/her if he/she will tell me if I seem to be behaving differently. I will note my signatures on letters, emails and personal accounts.

If there is a wide variation in any way I present myself, I do the following:
1. Notice any unusual bodily cues, gut feelings or thoughts.
2. Stay in the noticing; noting when I write or sign my name differently: Who am I writing to? What messages am I delivering? Where am I when I sign in that particular way?
3. Make notes in my journal.

The Meditation

Nourishment begins with accepting that my Present Self had no part in my past actions. Nourishment means stopping the thoughts or flashbacks as soon as I recognize an early cue. I replace them with a current thought.

I use the phrase, "I am here now and doing okay."

Notes

The Thought

Somewhere along the way I lost faith or was told I was not capable of having any faith.

Noticing & Awareness

For most of us trust and faith have always been given to someone we feel will take care of us, not control us. Notice when you have an uncomfortable or unexplainable bodily sensation which appears to respond to a person, place or thing. There is a distinct possibility that this discomfort is a signal of a conditioned response.

The Notion

Faith is about developing healthy and supportive belief systems about life and living in the present and future.

The Way Out

As I rediscover faith, I can trust myself and others more. I will need someone to trust.

The Meditation

I am still alive today because I have some sort of faith.

Today I will have faith in just one person, idea or belief. That person, idea or belief is:

_____

_____

_____

_____

_____

_____

_____

Notes

The Thought

"How can I support you?" often meant "This is what you are not allowed to do alone."

Noticing & Awareness

If you were overly controlled, conditioned or programmed as a child, lessons were not necessarily taught in the order a loving parent might naturally teach a young child.

Lessons on fear and safety may have been scrambled so that you did not have logical and usual healthy fears (i.e. a snake will bite me; fire can burn me) and instead you may have experienced illogical fears (i.e. water on my face as I shower; storms).

This exercise may trigger people and situations that put you at risk or that you believe tried to control or harm you at one time in your life. Try the first question of the six "who questions" in The Way Out section to see if you can remain in the present and evaluate people who are currently in your life.

The Notion

Regardless of whether programming was natural or purposeful as a child I was influenced by adults and other children. This influence impacted me both positively and negatively. I am now capable of asking for healthy support from the people I trust.

The Way Out

In my journal, I will make two lists:
List One: What I was not allowed to do or say.
List Two: What I have never asked anyone to help me accomplish.

I do not need to take any action on the lists. This is a clue to my personal conditioning, rules and regulations. I will stay in awareness and note if I feel physical symptoms or internally hear familiar sayings.

Here are six "who questions" for evaluating triggers, threats and any past threads.
1. Who are the current people in my life?
2. Who in my life am I clear about as to their purpose/motives?
3. Who in my life do I question as to their purpose/motives?
4. Who were the past important people in my life?
5. Who are the new people who enter my life, especially if they feel familiar?
6. Who has tried to befriend me recently and I did not allow him/her in?

The Meditation

I now redefine the meaning of support so that when someone I trust asks "What do I need to feel supported?" I can ask for what I want, need or desire.
Today I need:

_____

_____

Notes

The Thought

Numbers can trigger thoughts, feelings and actions.

Noticing & Awareness

Repetitions, memorization, sequencing, hypnosis and mnemonic devices are all forms of conditioned learning. Notice if you have a propensity for using one of these forms to learn new information. Notice if you have a better than average memory and what techniques you regularly use to remember information.

The Notion

I notice what the number seven (7) means: for example: days of the week, the number of chakras, colors of the rainbow, the virtues, and the number of classical planets. Conditioning or even memory improvement training consists of sequenced learning and anything common can be paired and conditioned.

The Way Out

I notice if I have an unusual attachment to the number seven (7).

Since conditioning and purposeful programming is often paired with uncommonly/rarely used scientific formulas, music scores, poetry verses, biblical verses and even your non-native language, stay in the noticing of sequences with sevens.

The Meditation

I accept that I may never understand the pairing and programming to common and uncommon things.

I do commit to remain in the noticing if a sequence causes me to think, feel or act differently than I expected. I accept that numbers, poetry, music, mathematical equations or sequences may mean something specific to me and trigger something which I may not understand.

Notes

The Thought

Others had me believe that unconditional love is defined by expectations.

Noticing & Awareness

If the words "unconditional love" trigger any uncomfortable feelings, continue to read this section and post the mediation somewhere you will be able to see it. Read it aloud and silently to yourself.

The Notion

Expectations are a normal part of being human. The trap is that an expectation can set me up for varied types of emotional backlash, specific disappointment and /or severe negative self talk.

The Way Out

Not doing everything I can to increase my self esteem allows others to control me. To increase my personal control over my life I:
1. Announce my expectations out loud when I hear them in my inner voices.
2. Write my expectations down and then review them to see if they align with present time and my current goals.
3. Put my list of expectations in several places because on a bad day, I might throw them away or misplace them.

The Meditation

I am aware that I have expectations.

I will stay in the awareness that expectations are only my wish that a person, situation or my self (selves) comply with a definition of the way it "should" be.

I now understand that not everything is controlled or turns out unpredictably.

I can manifest my heart's desire.

Notes

The Thought

What we all have done in common is layer ourselves. In purposeful programming the layers were chosen for me. I may never be able to know how many overcoats I wear or the number of multiple selves existing within.

Noticing & Awareness

Almost all programming is based on creating multiple personalities through splits. Some of this is done by abuse, fear and brainwashing techniques or by deep suggestions under the influence of mind altering drugs or hypnosis. If this section triggers discomfort, stop reading until you feel solid and observe the following:

Notice if you have an unusually styled wardrobe or clothing items that have an extreme variation in style. Notice if your wardrobe and surroundings have an excess of one color or void of color(s). Notice any extreme hobbies, or interests.

The Notion

Hearing committee voices and slight changes in behavior are normal. Thinking, speaking, dressing, behaving or acting like multiple people can signal a conditioned trigger. The point: we all have learned behaviors suitable for a particular situation; some of us were trained for behaviors suitable for a defined situation.

The Way Out

If I get a gut feeling or outright notice I am acting and speaking in an unusual way and/or it does not match the current situation, I do the following:
1. Use the STOP technique and ask myself: Am I in my Present Self?
2. Ask the question: Is my behavior, speech, dress and actions suitable for where I am now?
3. Record my answers in my journal.

The Meditation

The real me is in here.

I will continue to notice how he/she expresses himself/herself in the present. I use this information as a way back when I notice that I am "out" of my Present Self.

Notes

The Thought

I am an inexhaustible source of energy.

Noticing & Awareness

Inexhaustible source of energy has been identified in hypnosis scripts used to condition behavior. It is a precursor to creating altered personalities by interchangeably using the words delusion and illusion. The wording set up unimaginable human capacity and goals. The words "inexhaustible energy" are a trigger and are commonly used to push an individual's limits. It is quite possible that the suicide code in programming is built beneath this phrase.

Notice when you do not reasonably stop pushing yourself or push yourself too much or too far. If you feel any triggers, have a sense of going out of time and/or out of body, read The Meditation section.

The Notion

I need to explore and understand the difference between:
1. Pushing beyond my limits to achieve a new horizon and pushing to exhaustion.
2. Pushing beyond my current perceived capacity and pushing beyond a consciousness of the goals I set.

The Way Out

My body and my psyche have limits. I stay in the noticing of:

1. When am I exhausted?
2. When do I exhaust my friends?
3. When do I exhaust my family?
4. When do I exhaust my co-workers?

The Meditation

Each day I will take a few minutes to identify and list who and what remain a source of energy to me when I am exhausted.

_____

_____

_____

_____

_____

_____

_____

Notes

The Thought

Life experiences and conditioning gave me scripts about being enough.

Noticing & Awareness

Many of us have no concept of the word "enough". However, in conditioning or programming the word "enough" is tied to a script of an altered behavior. If you have a memory of physical or emotional starvation and/or indulgence, get your journal out and write about a time most recently when you felt you were enough and had enough.

You may notice in your everyday living that you either hoard or have become an exaggerated minimalist.

The Notion

The committee (all those real or imagined voices in my head) has judgments about my performance that range from desirable, good enough, enough to, not enough. In the present I remain aware that I continue to make judgments about being and having enough.

The Way Out

I am learning new definitions of the word "enough":
1. Enough means I set boundaries.
2. Enough does not equal that I push to the limit at all costs.
3. Enough does not equal that I consume as little as possible and stay starving.
4. Enough means I notice when the costs become too high physically, mentally, emotionally, intellectually or spiritually.
5. Enough means I notice what or who has caused me to override my sense of what I want or need in my Present Self.

The Meditation

I am always doing the best I can. I am always enough.

List some situations where I feel I can give enough and be enough.

_____

_____

_____

_____

_____

_____

Notes

The Thought

Keep peace at all costs.

Noticing & Awareness

The Thought section may trigger the following concept and memory:

Keeping peace at all costs is the conditioned version of "don't rock the boat." A phrase that may also be familiar to you is "blend in." Blending in is a highly developed skill of several forms of conditioning. If you are not famous, no one misses you if you disappear for a day or a year or forever. No one notices.

Believing any of these thoughts can block your personal or professional development and does not allow you to make decisions in the present.

The Notion

Negative self-talk coupled with fear and poor self image has conditioned me to blend in and not stand out.

Therefore, my intellect and creativity have remained undeveloped and unrecognized.

The Way Out

Cues and triggers that have a reoccurring pattern in my life can mean blend in and forget; keep peace and calm; don't rock the boat; keep a low profile.

Peace and calm are not always the goal nor are they desirable.

In my journal I make a list of:
1. Ways that I blend in.
2. How I keep peace and calm.
3. Where and with whom I do not rock the boat.
4. Where and with whom I keep a low profile.

The Meditation

I get to shine. I have a willful choice when I remain in my Present Self.

Places and situations where I feel comfortable being noticed or shinning are:

_____

_____

_____

_____

_____

Notes

The Thought

Selfish is a harsh word; a casually used word aimed directly at my heart intended to pierce it forever.

Noticing & Awareness

The word "obey" is a definite conditioning word and is the foundation for both the light side and the dark side of socialization. Those who received early rigid and punitive conditioning related to "obeying rules" can be instantly immobilized and controlled.

The Notion

I may have very well defined tapes of some adult telling me to share more, don't be such a pig! With the world constructed as it is, I cannot control all my encounters. I can, however, control how I react to those encounters.

The Way Out

I clearly set my limits of giving to others. I establish boundaries of what I will give back to others. I make a list of my needs and practice asking for what I need from those I trust.

Boundaries I may need to establish are:

_____

_____

_____

_____

_____

_____

_____

_____

The Meditation

I can give to others. My priority is to give to my self and be open to receive positive healing and abundance from others.

Some things I am willing to receive from others are:

_____

_____

_____

_____

Notes

The Thought

Abandonment felt like love, I knew it to be consistent from those who were keeping me alive.

Noticing & Awareness

In purposeful conditioning and programming, children learn self preservation by pretending not to care what happens to the one(s) they love the most. The inner voices say, "Closeness is dangerous." If no attachment is overtly shown, then those you love the most are not taken away or injured.

If this triggers a flashback or sense of fear, please stop reading and go to the Meditation section.

You might return another day to the topic of abandonment, so be gentle and forgiving in your Present Self.

The Notion

There are many psychological reasons for feeling abandoned. Most of which are defined by "being left." Being left behind, being left alone, being left with, being left to, being left out or just being left!

All of us have been left.

An inner belief is that "I am not enough to be chosen." I may recognize this as a reoccurring theme in my life that haunts and often cripples me at every turn.

The truth is somebody made a choice that wasn't right for me, but right for them at the time. Period. That's it. As piercing as this idea may feel, I was considered and then put in second place. Perhaps, worse, I was never considered at all.

The Way Out

The way out of this vicious circle is to declare what results I want. Now the work begins.

I will state what I do want, not what I don't want.

The Meditation

I deserve to have my heart's desire.

The results I want are:

_____

_____

_____

_____

_____

_____

Do not make a plan, do not have a strategy. Let new ways of having results show up.

Notes

The Thought

Suffocation is the opposite of abandonment. Think of them as twins. One or the other is triggered and they look alike. In my Soul they feel and burn alike.

Noticing & Awareness

The word "special" is used in this section and is one of the most potent trigger words for both conditioning and programming. It is used to make you comply. Learn to avoid people and situations where you are referred to as special. The word triggers separating and negative self talk and can have a spiral programming effect that sets off several other self belittling programs.

You may remember the word "special" pushes buttons for super human attempts at physical tasks.

Note in your journal how you feel when you say the word "special" aloud or silently to yourself.

The Notion

Suffocation goes something like this in our heads. I want you to come close, oops, not that close. Oh! Why are you going away? (abandoning me), I really want you to come closer. Sound a little schizophrenic? Well, yes and no. It was programmed to work that way.

Odd as it may sound, this becomes a normal way to invite people into my life. In building healthy relationships it is called "the dance."

Average people are predisposed to "dance" one way or the other because of the early relationships in life. These two triggered themes force me into a dance.

Is there a way out? Yes, there is.

The Way Out

Knowing I have a choice offers a way out. Do I want this person or thing in my life? Then I listen and follow my answer. Not all of us can do this. It will take courage. So where do I get that courage to listen and act?

I will believe that others care or should now. I am not special. Regardless of what Mother, Father, my spouse or my lover have told me, I am not special. Feeling special creates separateness from reality. My circle of trust can be as large or small as I choose.

The Meditation

I get to invite or uninvite others into my life space. I will pause for a moment and try to remember the last person who tried to enter my life space.
- What did I attach to the "why" they wanted to be in my life?
- How long did it take for me to feel safe that they would stay in my life?
- How long did it take for me to ask them to stay out of my life?
- If they didn't stay in my life, what reasons do I believe caused them to go away?

Notes

The Thought

"Let's make a deal" may mean random reward and punishment.

Noticing & Awareness

Doors are often used symbolically for conditioning new behaviors and for rewarding or punishing choices. Being placed in situations without any visible doors for long periods of time forces you to disappear into your Spirit. If you are reading this, congratulations! You were able to maintain your Present Self.

If any thoughts, feelings or beliefs are triggered go directly to The Meditation section.

The Notion

Doors can lead to trash or treasure; safety or danger. I may have memories of doors I wish I had never opened, and been forced to choose one in order to save myself or a loved one.

The Way Out

I can say no to doors now.

Identify:
1. What am I keeping alive?

  _____

  _____

2. What am I focusing on the most?

  _____

  _____

3. What am I neglecting?

  _____

  _____

4. What am I longing for?

  _____

  _____

5. What or who am/was I forced to choose between?

  _____

  _____

The Meditation

I embrace honor. I see two doors: one labeled healing and one labeled random. I am opening the door labeled healing and behind it is healing of all kinds. This is a form of healing I recognize and deserve. This is healing I had never imagined. I embrace healing now.

Notes

The Thought

Promises meant something would have a result. The result wasn't always what I expected.

Noticing & Awareness

If you feel agitated when you read this section, try slow breathing. If a promise is broken, someone could be hurt or even eliminated. The purpose of this section is to help your Present Self redefine the word "promise".

The Notion

I know what a false promise is in the world of triggers. In the present, promise means my word. It is all I own. When I set out to make a change, possessions and status guarantee nothing. I do so much better keeping promises to others than my "selves." The promises I make to my "selves" I often do not remember the next day. I start small. A promise kept means consistency, not perfection.

The Way Out

I start by:
1. Being consistent in what I feel, say, do, think and imagine.
2. Listening to myself when I speak about my desires and declarations of the results I want in my life.
3. Saying what I want; not still telling myself what I don't want or can't do.
4. Speaking kindly and encouragingly to myself.
5. Seeing myself having what I want.

The Meditation

I start my day by saying these three statements:
- I deserve a healing life.
- I deserve loving relationships.
- I deserve to rest, eat, sleep and play.

Notes

The Thought

Honesty, in the past, meant nothing as a word to me. Honesty, now, has a new definition in my Present Self.

Noticing & Awareness

The concept of honesty is addressed in this section. The word "honest" could trigger an instant disregard for developing intimacy in relationships. It is a layered program to keep a conditioned individual in the "non-deservingness" of meaningful relationships so he/she could be available without attachments and ready to "do the job."

If you feel strong disdain for the word honesty read this section three or four times.

The Notion

Honesty is the self-forgiveness that says OOPS! Let's start over. It's that little voice that belongs to Self who can say, "STOP! This is not working." Try another way. What follows next makes the difference in developing the foundation for self love or perpetuating the person who doesn't deserve love.

The Way Out

I am listening to the tone in which I stop myself when I am about to slip into an old pattern.

I may sound unkind and follow my thoughts with a trashing comment. Instead, I use a softer tone which reminds me that I don't have to be perfect all the time. I may never unravel all the threads that spark a slip into my old selves. Yet, by staying in the noticing, I continually learn the cues and signals leading up to a change or a trigger.

The Meditation

Close your eyes and imagine a baby trying to walk. We say...come on you can do it. We open our arms ready to catch the baby and if the baby falls, say OOPS! Good job! You can do it! We don't usually say...oh stupid baby you fell ...you are so dumb, you will never ever be able to take your first step.

A kindness to myself: Practice saying STOP to myself the way I say I LOVE YOU when I feel a familiar undesirable pattern emerging.

Then I remind myself that I am deserving of love and I repeat what I want as my heart's desire.

Notes

The Thought

Integrity can not be taught but it can be stolen.

Noticing & Awareness

This section offers a reconnection with the Present Self by reestablishing credibility and recognition of self in the present time. It can potentially trigger memories of names and places.

If you experience triggers, do either of the following: write all your names and places in your journal or say the name out loud. Then, repeat the following out loud: this name I remember is not me, my name is (add the name you are called today) and this is my Present Self.

The Notion

Integrity simply means I have no other choice. I said I would and I do. I do not quit, no matter how many times I have to start over. Over and over, I continue to shower myself with deserving thoughts and words, until one day I notice I am shouting the STOP! word in kindness.

The Way Out

There are four actions I take to reclaim my identity:
1. I decide how I will state my name when someone asks. I say it out loud.
2. I check the past for any alternative uses of my current name.
3. I Identify the time period and people in my life when I may have used an alternate for my present name.
4. If anyone calls me by another name, I will gently correct them and repeat my name clearly to them.

The Meditation

My Present Self is the keeper of my identity and integrity. I use my present name without variations or nicknames to remind myself of my true identity.

Do the following exercise:

Take a sheet of paper, draw a line down the middle – place your present name on the side of the sheet that corresponds with your dominant hand. Place your alternative names in the remaining column. Read the names out loud and notice if any names or variation of your name feel uncomfortable.

Notes

The Thought

Fear has a confidence band. I can even smell it.

Noticing & Awareness

Heightened sense of smell is a characteristic of conditioning which may have involved protection. Many are able to sense emotion through the sweat glands of others. Some can sense smells that trigger headaches, specific behavioral responses or programming. Still others can easily identify when someone enters a room or when someone had previously been in a room. Fear may have been paired with smells to activate a behavior without language or signaling.

The Notion

The word fear has long been defined as: <u>F</u>alse, <u>E</u>vidence, <u>A</u>ppearing <u>R</u>eal. In conditioning and programming false evidence, fear and truth were interchangeable concepts used to elicit desired outcomes. Behaviors are often presented in illogical order so that I could not figure out or predict the presenting situation. It may be why some therapeutic approaches have not addressed my needs.

The Way Out

There may be no logical sequence to what triggers fear for me. When I feel fear, the way out is:

1. Notice what or who is triggering that fear.
2. Assess any real danger. Leave or get help if the danger is real.
3. Control my thoughts, feelings or circumstances.
4. Eliminate having to be part of the situation.
5. Develop the best strategy to cope with the immediate threat if it cannot be eliminated.

The Meditation

I stay in the awareness of what is real and happening in the present. I note if I slipped into the past today. I note if there was evidence in the present to support feelings of fear? I ask myself "what appears so real that I am frightened to tell someone else?" or say it out loud to myself.

_____

_____

_____

_____

_____

_____

_____

_____

_____

Notes

The Thought

Blame is self hatred turned inward and programmed to crush my Spirit.

Noticing & Awareness

Blame triggers are thoughts such as: "I am not and never will be enough"; "I have lost all control because of them"; "I am lower than the lowest of all." Continue with this entire section and use the Meditation often.

The Notion

Effectively blaming my different selves is regulated negative self-talk that has formed a pattern of me doing the same things over and over until they are "enough." Remember we are conditioned and programmed never to be enough. This program says I am not enough. This vicious circle keeps my self-image under check. The programming of blame is built to trigger a self worth and self hatred tape. Self-hatred leads to self destruction, such as addiction, suicidal thoughts and abuse.

The Way Out

To support myself in eliminating this trigger I:
1. Eliminate negative self talk from my vocabulary.
2. Listen to myself talk to a friend on the phone, a salesperson in a store, someone at work. Am I using derogatory and self degrading comments?
3. Take stock of addictive behavior; seek help to assess it, control it or eliminate it.

The Meditation

- I am love and light now.
- I am a good and caring person.
- I deserve and have a right to receive love from those in my present life.

Notes

THE PAST

My past is comingled with my present. The best I can do is to have faith in the present and do what I can to remain in the Now of my life.

I am not my past. The past is over, good-bye.

The Thought

Some of us were taught to smell emotions. The fear I have smelled in others in the past has immobilized me in the present.

Noticing & Awareness

There are very physical and critical codes for anyone purposely programmed.

This section can trigger an instant physical response. If you notice any unusual physical sensations skip to the Way Out section.

The Notion

My senses are keener. I hear better, see better, smell better and taste better than most anyone else I know. Most say that's a blessing that allows me to fully experience the beauty of the world. However, for conditioned and programmed individuals it is a trigger.

The Way Out

The way out is to learn to separate me from others I perceive to be harmful. Observation is key here. I trust my gut. If I have a feeling or sensation, I ask myself these three simple questions:

1. Theirs or mine?
2. His or mine?
3. Hers or mine?

Leaving any situation or person that elicits a hypersensitive physical response is paramount to my health and well being; in fact, perhaps even my survival.

The Meditation

Breathe nine (9) deep breaths now.

I can retreat and remain separate from energy (people, places and situations) that negatively trigger me. I can and do walk away, speak out and leave any uncomfortable situation.

Notes

The Thought

I have changed everything else that reminded me of how I felt degraded, used, hurt and humiliated. I know I cannot change the past that I carry around each and every day.

Noticing & Awareness

This section can release tears and the feeling of a very deep cellular sadness. If you experience anger, know it is a cover for sadness. Take quiet time when you feel you can grieve for time lost. Remind yourself in the most loving way and with the kindest of words, that you are not your past. You are your present. Your future and you can remain in the Now.

The Notion

The past can surface at the most unexpected time for three reasons:
1. It is the common form to relate the experiences between two or more people.
2. It can be triggered by a specific memory or event as two or more people relate or remember an experience.
3. It can be triggered by a specific object, memory or event as you go through everyday personal experiences.

The Way Out

Releasing traumatic, uncomfortable or hurtful experiences requires that I create a circle of trust. This circle can consist of one or two people.

By practicing the STOP technique and reframing my thoughts, I can keep my mind and thoughts in the present. Contacting a trusted professional to work with restructuring and releasing my cellular memory is a valuable investment in reducing spontaneous triggering and staying in the Present Self.

The Meditation

The past is stored in my cells and my memories. Through practice and repetition I can soften and /or contain memories.

A good way to remain in my Present Self is to record a list of physical symptoms that I feel when I have a reoccurring memory or sense my Present Self is slipping away.

I practice saying:

◆ I am not my past.
◆ I am what I carry forward.
◆ I now choose willfully.

Notes

The Thought

I do not need fixing. I was tricked into believing I was never enough.

Noticing & Awareness

The "fixing me" principle is conditioned/programmed very early, so that negative self talk or directives on how to be "better" could be easily embedded and inserted into any required task or assignment. If this concept triggers a feeling of lack of self esteem, a sense of shame or an urge to work harder at an existing task, use the STOP technique. Then remind yourself that you are in control of what you want to change.

The Notion

I may exhibit an unexplainable willingness to participate in attacking my" selves" or others for some unknown reason. My memories of past behaviors often bleed through when I am looking for the "fix." I may have been told I am schizophrenic, paranoid, a liar and a loser.

The Way Out

When I feel I need "fixing" I make a list.

What needs "fixing?"

_____

_____

What are the reason(s) this needs to be "fixed?"

_____

_____

How does "fixing it "contribute to my future?

_____

_____

Do I have any negative thoughts about myself?

_____

_____

Does this support or erode my heart's desire?

_____

_____

The Meditation

I no longer accept someone else's evaluation of my needs unless I am specifically asking for his/her evaluation or help.

Notes

THE PRESENT

Identifying safe people in my life helps keep me in the present. I use safe people as sounding boards, reality checks and confidants.

I stay in my Present Self.

The Thought

I can stay in focus today...if even for one fraction of a moment.

Noticing & Awareness

Stay with this page until you can read the entire section. It may take you several reads. Laughter is a good response to this trigger.

The Notion

Whether or not I have ever experienced intense programming and control, without practice I can shift my focus repeatedly through the day. Add significant triggers and not only am I shifting focus, I may end up wondering where did the time go? How did I get here? What was my original goal/plan?

The Way Out

To remain in the Present Self I will:
1. Wear a watch.
2. Divide my day into quarters: Waking to Noon: Noon to 6pm: 6pm to Sleep: Sleep to Waking.
3. Notice at which periods I lose focus the most.
4. Notice the periods where I am most fearful.
5. Notice the periods where I am feeling safest.

The Meditation

◆ I am here in this time; in this place - now.
◆ I breathe nine slow deliberate breaths.
◆ I repeat with each breath the phrase:" I am in the present."

Notes

The Thought

Everyday I choose to come one step closer to my Present Self.

Noticing & Awareness

Sounds, including music will trigger all kinds of memories, regardless of natural or purposeful programming. Keep ongoing notes in your journal of what sounds seem to trigger reoccurring thoughts and/or particular behaviors. Many programmed individuals will be triggered by common household sounds, especially the ringing of a phone; the on/off cycles of the refrigerator and the alarm clock.

The Notion

I may feel I cannot escape the world I currently live in unless I opt out. Intentionally using the everyday sounds and the sounds I hear internally can give me a way to eliminate any external signals to trigger or activate me. Knowing common cues and triggers as well as my personal set of triggers provides me a way to refocus to the present. I have a highly developed sense of hearing.

The Way Out

I practice going from one frequency (vibration) to another by:
- Singing songs, humming, chanting or even focusing on non-triggering colors. All of these can also be a trigger; so unless I am clear and have identified related triggers, I do not use any of these.
- Listening to any sound in my immediate surroundings and imagine it sounding louder or quieter.
- Assessing what I feel like when I hear these sounds.

The Meditation

I already know how to change vibrations; it is coded in my Soul. It is part of my genetics. It is primal to my Being. It is my way out.

Notes

The Thought

I start a new phase in my life. I remember that I do not have to repent.

Noticing & Awareness

The word "repent" definitely sets off triggers. It means pay back beyond extraordinary means. Continue to read this section and if you identify extreme measures of giving or giving back to others, carry this meditation with you; read it frequently.

The Notion

I don't have to make excuses for anyone else. I don't have to change for anyone else. I don't have to fix anyone else.

Everyday I am given the opportunity to begin again and to let go of my past the second after it happens. But I may not be able to remain in the present and express my disappointment, my hurt, my fear and even my joy. I stuff it. In my case I may have been taught to stuff. I stuffed without memory. I stuffed for survival.

The Way Out

I repeat each day as often as necessary:

I am capable of being a loving deserving person.

The Meditation

Each day I have a choice.

- I can remain in the past or start anew.
- I can choose a past to carry as my burden.
- I can create a new beginning that moves me towards my Present Self.
- I choose Now.

Today I chose:

_____

_____

_____

_____

_____

_____

_____

Notes

The Thought

I want to get out of the "tornado" and to love this person inside of me.

Noticing & Awareness

Tornado is a trigger word. If it is a trigger word for you, skip to the Meditation section. Continue on a daily basis for at least three weeks to do all the meditation sections up to this page, before you try reading The Notion again.

The Notion

Cueing up the phrase" I do not have a healthy self" is a trap for creating illness both mentally and physically. Identifying as the "Doer" is a trap. Identifying as the "Dreamer" is the trap. "Desirer" was the forbidden.

The Way Out

The escape is to remain in the Present Self.

The Meditation

The person inside of me is the one who has contributed to my survival and I can call on him/her for good. I acknowledge myself for being and/or doing the following:

_____

_____

_____

_____

_____

_____

_____

_____

_____

Notes

The Thought

Nowhere did I ever, or do I now, deserve lies.

Noticing & Awareness

Discerning fact and fiction is unusually difficult for gifted and highly conditioned and programmed individuals who were/are developed and trained to see no barriers, obstacles or potential for personal injury. It triggers a memory in your gut when you are in the presence of someone not telling the truth. A voice inside you screams.

When it comes to knowing the truth, value and trust your gut; it has saved your life and the lives of others. Words and actions have not always been truthful if you were purposely programmed.

The Notion

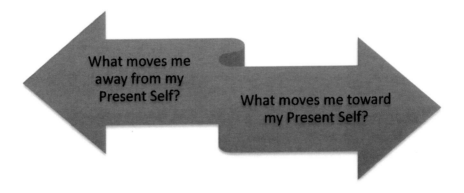

What moves me away from my Present Self?

What moves me toward my Present Self?

The Way Out

The goal is to move toward the heart's desire of my Present Self through the persistence, practice and patience of beginning again after I have an altered experience.

I make a list of what keeps me moving towards my Present Self and what keeps me moving away. I listen to my head and my heart.

Moving Towards:

_____

_____

_____

_____

Moving Away:

_____

_____

_____

_____

The Meditation

Everyday I am recognizing and becoming friends with my Present Self.

Notes

The Thought

I will stay committed to my Present Self.

Noticing & Awareness

A new meaning for the word "commitment" is introduced in this section. The word commitment triggers a double edged command- "stay on task and get your job done" and "never, ever commit to anyone unless instructed to do so."

You will learn to approach and redefine commitment in a way that gives you control over what and who enters your life space.

The Notion

Commitment is making a positive choice to be fully where I am now. It is very different from affirmations which focus on beliefs that may not be true yet or make no sense if I look beyond conditioning or programming.

The Way Out

I am now declaring out loud what I choose. These declarations stem from my "value words" not from my trigger words. Value phrases are my constant reminders that I am an active participant in this thing called life. Some examples of value phrases are: I matter; I am worth it; I am loveable: I deserve good; I am worthy of receiving.

The Meditation

I do believe that I have enough inner strength and power to overcome any programming or conditioning that was used without my consent.

Three signs of my inner strength in my everyday present life are:

1. _____

2. _____

3. _____

Notes

The Thought

As I attempt to change my path, it suddenly feels like I have a multitude of selves.

Noticing & Awareness

We may not know what we are capable of doing, or what we are capable of not doing. To create a new memory map it is important to remain in your Present Self and assign close friends the job of confirming your courage. Remember you are alive today because your Spirit has never abandoned you and because of a grace you may never understand.

The Notion

When I successfully alter one response, it is a sign that I am capable of altering my entire set of responses. In the greater picture, it means I am fully capable of being positive in this world and making conscious decisions based on what is occurring in the present.

The Way Out

I will not quit on myself. I have more strength than I realize. I have survived to this day through my strength, creativity and grace.

The Meditation

I love my Present Self enough to continue, no matter what it takes, I can do this.

I commit to one activity each day to continue living in my Present Self. (it is ok for me to list the same activity more than once):

Sunday: _____

Monday: _____

Tuesday: _____

Wednesday: _____

Thursday: _____

Friday: _____

Saturday: _____

Notes

The Thought

I may be tempted to explain myself to people.

Noticing & Awareness

The trigger might be the memory when you were required "to explain yourself." The word "explain" is also a single word trigger used to put someone on defense or provide detailed information about an event or task.

The Notion

A fear is that I better not tell anyone about who I think I am/or may have been in the past. Surely they will think me crazy. I believe at times that I must therefore lie and deceive others at all costs.

The Way Out

Announcing publicly the impact and effects of my conditioning or programming is not generally what most of us are willing to do. It requires a foundation and development of ego strength that can handle rejection, attack and the discrediting of self worth. Our reputation may be endangered.

I remember these two simple mantras:

- It is none of anyone else's business what and who I might have been at anytime in my life.
- I trust that I will intuitively know who to tell among friends, family and lovers.

The Meditation

I do not owe anyone explanations about my life. It is perfectly acceptable and even quite valuable to gently and calmly say: I do not want to discuss that with you.

List two phrases you can use when you prefer not to discuss an aspect of your life:

1. _____

2. _____

Notes

The Thought

I am willing, able and prepared to stand in the attack. It is the only way I will ever know what anyone fears about me.

Noticing & Awareness

The word "attack" is a trigger word. It is one of the most familiar trigger words to conditioned and programmed individuals.

Read this entire section at least twice.

The Notion

The fear of leaving behind a comfortable story about my past is, at times, immobilizing. My story is sometimes so frightening that I would rather drive myself into illness, disease and even death.

So what does standing in the attack look like in real life? First of all it isn't easy and it's not hard. It's just different. It requires a real shift out of a need to be right or make someone else wrong: a shift away from blame, away from excuses into compassion.

As soon as I hear the words of blame flowing from my mouth I will lovingly say "STOP." I will "STOP" for a moment. I notice my reaction so it teaches me what I've been stuffing. What I blame the most in others is what I stuff the most in myself.

The Way Out

Observe any patterns by identifying: Who was I with? What was I doing? Where was I at?
1. When I stuffed when I wanted to speak?
2. When I disappeared when I really wanted to be seen?
3. When I remained silent and did not get to say enough?
4. When someone cut me off?

Now reflect on this question:

What do I stand for in the present time?

_____

_____

_____

_____

_____

_____

The Meditation

My life is reflective of what I believe in and value most. I do not need to explain myself to others.

Notes

The Thought

I can use "cues" to override past suggestions and to create my new and own internal responses.

Noticing & Awareness

Continue to notice if you are moving unconsciously through your day. Slowly notice by the half day when you are most and least conscious. Then notice hour by hour when you are most aware. Note in your journal by drawing a line down the center of a page with the headings Most Conscious and Least Conscious.

The Notion

Cues can be anchored and/or paired with anything. Everyone has responses based on cues being triggered. Cues can be purposefully suggested or programmed to elicit a behavior or set of behaviors.

As I become more aware of what cues trigger me, I can begin to consciously create my own cues for greater freedom and choice.

The Way Out

"Cues" in the past always equaled external control. I can now recognize cues, eliminate them and use the STOP technique or reframing process to stay in the present.

The top five cues I will notice and practice eliminating with the STOP technique are:

1. _____

2. _____

3. _____

4. _____

5. _____

The Meditation

I can and do remain conscious. I now have more choice about my life's decisions and direction.

Notes

The Thought

My hyper vigilant body is really my friend asking for acknowledgement and participation in my life.

Noticing & Awareness

Your body may signal you when an unexpected or unconscious cue presents itself. Note how your body feels when you are alone, with family, with friends and in social gatherings. If you feel hyper vigilant in any of these situations, your body needs to be thanked for calling out to you. If this occurs, remain in the present and remind yourself who you are with and where you are at. Then decide if you want to leave.

The Notion

Others are too busy worrying about themselves to always acknowledge and encourage me. The job is mine. For those who have been programmed to discount feelings and emotions or are triggered inappropriately, this job seems impossible. As a result, little or no inner validation comes my way. I have the ability to change how I respond to feelings and emotions.

The Way Out

I can learn to know the triggers; understand the non-productive or debilitating thoughts produced, and successfully interrupt the acting out of undesirable behavior. I can reframe what I desire in the present. I can construct a new thought and begin as many times as necessary.

The Meditation

I will use one minute every night to positively acknowledge myself. After thirty (30) days of practice, I will acknowledge myself throughout the day.

Ten (10) ways I can positively acknowledge myself:

1. _____

2. _____

3. _____

4. _____

5. _____

6. _____

7. _____

8. _____

9. _____

10. _____

Notes

The Thought

I am not my body. Escaping my body's feelings was and is my way out of torturous thoughts.

Noticing & Awareness

If this section triggers body memory, note where and how your body is responding and continue reading.

The Notion

Everyone has felt a sense of being abandoned, suffocated or rejected. Most of these translate into anger, fear, sadness or blame. No one escapes these feelings growing up. Yet I may have been taught how to integrate them into my life so that I presented myself with less emotion.

The key concept is: A core emotion is layered with multiple interpretations. Once I recognize that I have layers of interpretations (mine and others) then I am open to freeing myself and moving forward.

The Way Out

For anyone who continues to experience painful memories through body sensations, the way to begin to quiet the memories is to thank your body for the memory.

Lovingly I say to myself: This is the past, I can quiet down this self talk a little at a time and let go.

The Meditation

I remain centered and aware in my body. I am safe in the present.

How I feel safe in the present:

_____

_____

_____

_____

_____

_____

_____

_____

Notes

The Thought

What value was placed on my body? What value do I now place on my body?

Noticing & Awareness

You may experience a number of responses to thinking about the value of your body, particularly in abuse programming.

Do not get tired, hungry or stressed. Your body can take over and revert to programming under those conditions.

Breathe deeply a few times and then continue reading this section. If memories are too overwhelming after you stop to breathe, go to the next page.

The Notion

I keep my word by following through each time I said I would or acknowledging to myself and others that I have changed plans. I increase the chance of staying in touch with my body when I do something I said I would do. My mind through thoughts and feelings is so connected to my body that unless I become aware of the triggers and cues about body worthiness, severe internal judgment will discard my worth as an individual.

The Way Out

I am not my body.

My body has been the carrier of my conditioning and programming.

I now listen and identify the messages my body sends to me so that when I feel these messages I can use the STOP technique and remain in my Present Self.

The Meditation

Each night as I am preparing for bed, I ask myself about my day's activities.

Did this activity give me value?

If yes, I write down the activity and use it to remain in the present.

_____

_____

_____

If no, I identify the trigger or sensations I noticed just before the activity, during the activity and after the activity; and then use the STOP technique to assess and control/eliminate this activity.

_____

_____

_____

Notes

The Thought

I am afraid of what would happen if people really knew me or worse yet, could hear my thoughts.

Noticing & Awareness

The Notion section will feel very familiar if you have never intimately shared any of your past. Your conditioned past is just that- a past- and one that new conversations can change.

The horrific nature of some past /current programmed behaviors is too fearful for the average person to even entertain thinking about; let alone accepting that these experiences may have happened to someone they love. The reality is that unless it is cult related, most people are not capable of understanding someone who was programmed against his/her will. Most people do not have the capacity to make a difference even if you do share your past.

The Notion

At times we all have thoughts and feelings that alarm us. The thoughts and feelings seem to have nothing to do with what is taking place before my eyes and in the present. I may feel that sharing these thoughts could ruin my reputation, alienate family and friends or put my life at jeopardy.

The Way Out

I cannot tell most people my experiences. If they have not lived a similar past, they have absolutely no understanding of my experiences. I can trust a compassionate, caring friend. I will trust someone with my past.

The Meditation

There are some of my life experiences I bury. I acknowledge my sadness in being unable to fully share. There are private secrets all people keep regardless of their past.

The people in my life I can trust to share my secrets are:

_____

_____

_____

_____

_____

Notes

The Thought

Peace and harmony are not the only goals. I am not afraid to disturb peace and harmony and open Pandora's Box of possibilities.

Noticing & Awareness

Everyone fears opening Pandora's Box. Please read this entire section and if you need to avoid the "box", allow yourself this thought: I can avoid this box and will mentally open it in a place and time where whatever is inside has lost its control over me.

The Notion

Someone, everyone tampers with the box. The box is always conditioned/programmed to be triggered. It may be my fear and thoughts that allow the triggers to progress and control my life without conscious choice.

The Way Out

The dilemma is: open the box and risk memories and/or flashbacks; don't open the box, risk living in fear and hostage thoughts forever. The reality is my boxes are open all the time; the boxes are conditioned and programmed to be triggered by common and everyday cues. The way out is to create my own boxes.

I take a small box and every time I have a past negative memory, I write it down immediately and put it in the box. Once a month I burn the box containing all the memories. I may find that I put many of the same memories in the box for several months.

It is okay to repeat the process as many times as needed.

The Meditation

Healing is not about creating positive thoughts, healing is about assessing, controlling, breaking and eliminating old thoughts and restoring that space created with a present thought that lovingly defines who I am in my Present Self.

Old Thoughts

_____

_____

_____

_____

_____

New Thoughts

_____

_____

_____

_____

_____

Notes

The Thought

I believe some things and not other things about my "selves."

Noticing & Awareness

In this handbook positive affirmations are not advocated as a technique to impact programming and conditioning. Positive affirmations that are not true in the present can feed into illusion/delusional programming that can keep you confused. This can keep you confused on what is real in the present and what may be a hallucination from the past.

If this position is not aligned with your personal belief system at this time, skip this section entirely.

The Notion

There are many ways to go about this work and one of them is to go into denial and fear. Pretending I am someone I have not become yet. When I feed myself with positive affirmations that aren't true, my inner self says - nonsense! and rejects them. Instead, the way out is to begin to ask for my heart's desire and take actions in the present to notice what and who supports my desires Now.

The Way Out

I write down my own beliefs about my Present Self. I read these messages to myself out loud to determine if this is what I believe in the present. I continue to record my beliefs until they are reflective of the present.

The Meditation

I am the most powerful re-programmer of my beliefs. I say what is true now and I ask for my heart's desire in the days ahead.

Ten things that I know are true about myself now are:

1. _____

2. _____

3. _____

4. _____

5. _____

6. _____

7. _____

8. _____

9. _____

10. _____

Notes

The Thought

It is always okay for me to need, want, and/or desire in the present.

Noticing & Awareness

This section focuses on releasing yourself from deprivation caused by conditioning and/or programming. Learning the early cues of deprivation is critical when you want to stop unconscious behavior.

The Notion

The key is to focus and refocus on the thought in the present, regardless of how many times I have to stop backsliding into the thoughts of the past. I focus and refocus on my present surroundings.

The Way Out

Intention plus attention equals different ways of moving through the world. I use the STOP technique as soon as I recognize an early cue. I remind myself of what I do want and then take inventory to determine if am functioning and making choices in my Present Self.

The Meditation

Using a blank calendar; my Outlook, Blackberry or datebook I schedule a month's worth of fifteen (15) minute appointments with me. During those fifteen (15) minutes I focus on what I notice wherever I happen to be during my appointment times. I acknowledge any visual triggers and remove them. I can trash them and take them right to the garbage can. Regardless of how much attachment or how long I have had any item, I can now recognize a trigger and choose to control it or eliminate it.

How I envision myself after twelve months:

_____

_____

_____

_____

_____

_____

_____

_____

_____

_____

_____

Notes

The Thought

Is there anyone or anything still hurting me?

Noticing & Awareness

The trigger that may occur here is the phrase "the hand that heals is the same hand that can kill." It is what the destruct program taught highly programmed individuals to do: get the job/ task at hand complete at all costs and then heal your own self so no one notices.

For those who have been attracted to healing and or massage therapy as a profession, you may realize that you are unable to do any "hands on" work because of a sensitivity to energy or even your past memories of heal/kill.

The Notion

Where my body hurts is a clue. Many conditioned individuals have the ability to self heal and to understand energy work. I pay attention to my clues.

The Way Out

What I continue to think and say about my past can hurt me.

If I begin to feel hurt, emotionally or physically, I will:
- Acknowledge the pain and discomfort.
- Check to see if the pain or discomfort truly needs to be addressed medically and/or psychologically.
- Put these thoughts or feelings into a box to look at later.
- Think or say something different about my self in the present.

I mentally record any places that hurt on my body when I feel I am having flashbacks or blocked memories from the past. I can draw a body outline below and label parts of my body that have unusual sensations.

The Meditation

My hands and heart intend healing for myself and others.
Three ways that I heal myself or help others heal:

1. _____

2. _____

3. _____

Notes

The Thought

Is there anyone or anything I have a memory of trying to protect?

Noticing & Awareness

You may feel your body go into a hyper vigilant mode when you read The Notion section. The way out is to notice and do not let the thought or memory move you into recreating the experience. If you feel an abundance of body tension, skip the activity suggested in The Way Out section.

The Notion

All of us take on the responsibility to protect someone or something. It is conditioned in me naturally and also a programming technique.

The Way Out

Do the following:
1. List the people and the social causes that mean the most to me in the present.
2. Identify ways I protect these people and causes.
3. Determine if any of my behaviors match any triggers I am aware of or have identified thus far.
4. List any projects/secrets/ideas I sense I am protecting.

The Meditation

I cannot always rely on my memory as a pathway to the positive choices I wish to make in the present. I give myself permission each day to continue to choose positively in the present.

Notes

The Thought

How is this serving me?

Noticing & Awareness

Before beginning this section, take time to write out your definition of the words "serve" and "servant." Next, think about the people in your life now. Write down their names and next to each name assess if you feel you serve him/her or if you are a servant to him/her. When you complete this, please continue to read this section.

Serve means:

Servant means:

Name	Serve	Servant

The Notion

If I find myself feeling or being treated like a servant around others, then I look to see if there is a disconnect between genuine giving to those I love. If there is a disconnect, I question the extent to which I truly believe I am being used and /or abused. I may not always know where to draw the line of helping and serving.

The Way Out

- I invite in what will serve me.
- I remember that the feeling of being a servant means some form of conditioning or control.
- When I serve others I do so by choice.
- I have a choice.

The Meditation

I am not a servant. I am here to serve my Present Self and support others who I know, love and trust.

Ways I enjoy serving others:

_____

_____

_____

_____

_____

_____

Notes

The Thought

I "get to get" beliefs do have past definitions of limitations, conditions and controls. My Present Self now creates what serves me.

Noticing & Awareness

Deprivation is a well-known form of conditioning, programming and brainwashing. You may have memories of never being able to ask for anything, including basic survival needs. Deprivation memories also access coded fear. Am I or will I ever be enough?

As I read this section I stop and say to myself as many times as necessary, "I get to get."

The Notion

The false notion is that if I take care of myself first, then I am really selfish. I am not supposed to ask for anything for myself. A well conditioned thought is: someone will give it to me if I need it. Variations of the same conditioning theme are: if I really do need it, someone will notice; if I work hard enough, I'll get it and, finally, I don't need or deserve it.

The Way Out

Asking in the present is limited by my fear, experiences, memories and imagination or the suggestions and conditioning I received in the past. I get to ask for what I desire.

The Meditation

◆ Thank you for that which is necessary for the fulfillment of my divine plan and all that I could ever desire.

I post the above meditation in a place where I can read it daily.

What I desire and deserve in the present is:

_____

_____

_____

_____

_____

_____

_____

Notes

The Thought

Honesty is self-forgiveness that says" OOPS"! Let me begin again.

Noticing & Awareness

Highly conditioned and programmed individuals are master manipulators because they have been programmed to have no regard for honesty and trust. You may struggle with where and with whom these concepts fit and how they play out in your world.

The Notion

Honesty and trust are two very different words in the conditioned world. You may have memories of only having one chance and then there were illogical and/or irrational consequences. What is chosen does not always make logical sense in the results produced. Therefore, honesty and trust can become confusing words often resulting in going against our innate integrity.

The Way Out

The way out is to talk as gently to myself as I would a small child.

All I can humanly do is turn down the volume on my past and commit to staying in the present.

The Meditation

I can start over as many times as I want to begin again. This is a gift of healing which I accept for myself in the present.

Who do I believe I can count on? And what can I count on him/her for?

_____

_____

_____

_____

_____

_____

_____

_____

_____

Notes

The Thought

"What do I stand for?" Is a question that can be a real diversion.

Noticing & Awareness

There is no longer a requirement to stand up for ourselves. This is a trigger phrase and equivalent to the word "Why?" It places us in a defensive position, looking for past experiences to justify our present behavior. The result is we get lost in past memories and most likely past triggers trying to defend our present beliefs and actions.

The Notion

Standing up for something keeps me in the state of self defense, thus depleting me of the joy and pleasure of the present. It can deplete my immune system and make me ill. If I spend a lot of time and energy standing up for myself, I have no time left for being in the present.

The Way Out

The way out is to know what matters and what has importance in my life now. I will do the following:

1. Define where I am and how I feel now.
2. Ask myself if this is an honest assessment of now.
3. Think about and write down what I want and my heart's desire now.
4. Verbalize aloud my heart's desire.
5. Ask my Present Self: Does this serve me now and how does this matter now?

The Meditation

I remind my Present Self as often as possible that I am willing to keep moving toward the inquiry and action that brings me to my heart's desire.

Notes

The Thought

Regardless of whoever I was, what road I have traveled or where I was born, I have a light and dark self. It is a human and lifesaving condition.

Noticing & Awareness

The side of love and light is surely equal, if not greater than the side of darkness.

The light self and the dark self is our internal check and balance system that brought us to where we are today. That is our constant companion in the present and our guide in the future. While we may feel guilt, shame, confusion, sadness or anger at having been manipulated into the dark side of life, this section reminds you that you did not deserve to be shamed for this split.

As you reclaim your Present Self, you reclaim the gift of knowing both sides.

The Notion

A primal and universal question for all humankind, regardless of conditioning or programming is: If people really knew me...how would they react ...would they love me? The fear is: Could I ever become more evil than good, having been conditioned to shame?

The Way Out

The way out is to know in my mind, in my heart, and in every cell of my Being, that I do not willingly and knowingly ever choose the dark side. In this place of Present Self, in this place of choice and in this place of moving forward, I am always surrounded by the light and the dark.

When I remain conscious, I always have a choice. I release the thoughts that hold me hostage. I change the conversation.

In my Present Self I chose the light.

The Meditation

I am a song of blessings and in my Present Self I continue to choose to live in love and light that I so richly deserve and desire to bring to others.

Notes

The Thought

My heart's desire for you, Dear Reader:

Stay true to the struggle and the inquiry to identify and live in your Present Self.

I know with full certainty that you can exchange your struggle for discovery. You have the strength and the grace to change the conversation and let go of the thoughts that hold you hostage.

You have the right to remain in your Present Self and live more freely in the moment.

You did not have a choice then.

You have a choice now.

Your Spirit has never abandoned you.

REVIEW

Using the list of Thoughts in the review section, you can check the Thoughts you want to review and/or focus on over the next months. As you review, you might want to add new ways out and some personal meditations.

THE HABITS   Pages 1 to 18

- ☐ Eight basic conditions of a habit form the groundwork to help control and/or eliminate conditioning and programming.
- ☐ Momentum: A habit gains momentum each time it is practiced.
- ☐ Reversion: The tendency to revert to a familiar and often unproductive habit increases when I am tired, hungry, stressed or angry.
- ☐ Awareness: I stay in the noticing and awareness of what precedes or triggers the habit.
- ☐ Short Circuiting: To change or discard a habit I need to be aware of the habit and all the properties surrounding the habit.
- ☐ Decisions and Selectiveness: I live in the willingness to release the habit and accept it back if it is useful. I am selective.
- ☐ Practice: Habits are predictable and predictably unpredictable and can be altered with committed, even relentless practice. Practice is a lifelong art.
- ☐ Trust: All the education in the Universe won't necessarily make a difference for some habits. Sometimes it is a matter of just trusting the process.

Thoughts for Review

THE THOUGHTS   Pages 19 to 28

- ☐ My duty was programmed, my desire is willful.
- ☐ I simply cannot continue down a spiritual path struggling to stay "in control". It is bigger than that.
- ☐ The way out of control is not always equal to the way I was conditioned or programmed into control.
- ☐ I do not need fixing. My past brings me to this day and who I am now.

THE COMMITTEE   Pages 29 to 38

- ☐ There are always, I repeat, always, voices speaking.
- ☐ I can learn to manage the committee in my head with my Present Self.
- ☐ I am committed to having new conversations with others and the Committee voices in my head.
- ☐ I can learn to vibrate above the chatter of the committee and all other internal and external sounds.

THE SCRIPTS Pages 39 to 80

- ☐ I know the meaning of autopilot. I do, however, often forget where the plane is headed.
- ☐ I may not know the recipe. What I do know is that all recipes can be modified.
- ☐ I do not know many others who are capable of understanding and nourishing my many "selves."
- ☐ Somewhere along the way I lost faith or was told I was not capable of having any faith.
- ☐ "How can I support you?" often meant "This is what you are not allowed to do alone."
- ☐ Numbers can trigger thoughts, feelings and actions.
- ☐ Others had me believe that unconditional love is defined by expectations.
- ☐ What we all have done in common is layer ourselves. In purposeful programming the layers were chosen for me. I may never be able to know how many overcoats I wear or the number of multiple selves existing within.
- ☐ I am an inexhaustible source of energy.
- ☐ Life experiences and conditioning gave me scripts about being enough.

Thoughts for Review

THE SCRIPTS (cont'd)

- ☐ Keep peace at all costs.
- ☐ Selfish is a harsh word; a casually used word aimed directly at my heart intended to pierce it forever.
- ☐ Abandonment felt like love, I knew it to be consistent from those who were keeping me alive.
- ☐ Suffocation is the opposite of abandonment. Think of them as twins. One or the other is triggered and they look alike. In my Soul they feel and burn alike.
- ☐ "Let's make a deal" may mean random reward and punishment.
- ☐ Promises meant something would have a result. The result wasn't always what I expected.
- ☐ Honesty, in the past, meant nothing as a word to me. Honesty, now, has a new definition in my Present Self.
- ☐ Integrity can not be taught but it can be stolen.
- ☐ Fear has a confidence band. I can even smell it.
- ☐ Blame is self hatred turned inward and programmed to crush my Spirit.

Thoughts for Review

THE PAST   Pages 81 to 88

- [ ] Some of us were taught to smell emotions. The fear I have smelled in others in the past has immobilized me in the present.
- [ ] I have changed everything else that reminded me of how I felt degraded, used, hurt and humiliated. I know I cannot change the past that I carry around each and every day.
- [ ] I do not need fixing. I was tricked into believing I was never enough.

THE PRESENT   Pages 89 to 138

- [ ] I can stay in focus today...if even for one fraction of a moment.
- [ ] Everyday I chose to come one step closer to my Present Self.
- [ ] I start a new phase in my life. I remember that I do not have to repent.
- [ ] I want to get out of the "tornado" and to love this person inside of me.
- [ ] Nowhere did I ever, or do I now, deserve lies.
- [ ] I will stay committed to my Present Self.

Thoughts for Review

THE PRESENT (cont'd)

- ☐ As I attempt to change my path, it suddenly feels like I have a multitude of selves.
- ☐ I may be tempted to explain myself to people.
- ☐ I am willing, able and prepared to stand in the attack. It is the only way I will ever know what anyone fears about me.
- ☐ I can use "cues" to override past suggestions and to create my new and own internal responses.
- ☐ My hyper vigilant body is really my friend asking for acknowledgement and participation in my life.
- ☐ I am not my body. Escaping my body's feelings was and is my way out of torturous thoughts.
- ☐ What value was placed on my body? What value do I now place on my body?
- ☐ I am afraid of what would happen if people really knew me or worse yet, could hear my thoughts.
- ☐ Peace and harmony are not the only goals. I am not afraid to disturb peace and harmony and open Pandora's Box of possibilities.
- ☐ I believe some things and not other things about my "selves."

THE PRESENT (cont'd)

- ☐ It is always okay for me to need, want, and/or desire in the present.
- ☐ Is there anyone or anything still hurting me?
- ☐ Is there anyone or anything I have a memory of trying to protect?
- ☐ How is this serving me?
- ☐ I "get to get" beliefs do have past definitions of limitations, conditions and controls. My Present Self now creates what serves me.
- ☐ Honesty is self-forgiveness that says" OOPS"! Let me begin again.
- ☐ "What do I stand for?" Is a question that can be a real diversion.
- ☐ Regardless of whoever I was, what road I have traveled or where I was born, I have a light and dark self. It is a human and lifesaving condition.
- ☐ My heart's desire for you, Dear Reader:
  Stay true to the struggle and the inquiry to identify and live in your Present Self.

My Personal Thought Template

You can use the blank template on the following page for any Thoughts you want to develop on your own. I can also email you a copy of the Thought Template.

Please email your request to mypresentself@gmail.com

The Thought

Thought:

_____

_____

_____

Noticing & Awareness

The Notion

148

The Way Out

The Meditation

Notes

About the Author

Nan Brenzel was born in Pennsylvania and earned her doctorate in counseling and research from West Virginia University. She has practiced the healing arts and meditation for over 50 years. Nan teaches the impact of journaling, movement, martial arts, Qigong, Reiki and nutrition on decision-making. She combines self talk, silence, meditation and movement with intense and compassionate coaching to assess, control, break or eliminate the conversation and thoughts which sabotage our ability to find and live more fully in our Present Self.

She is committed to creative coaching environments where beliefs, values, ideals and dreams of varied and distinct backgrounds can be developed into models which positively impact on socioeconomic and sociological conditions worldwide.

Nan's experience has included individual coaching and intensive retreats internationally for executives, administrators, professional athletes, religious communities, human service providers, non-profit agencies, hospitals, parents and educators.

If you have any questions, thoughts to share, or want to schedule a coaching session, intensive or a retreat, please email me at: mypresentself@gmail.com . You are invited to visit my website at www.resultpath.net for updates on upcoming events.

In Love and Light,
Nan